Making Science Work

Finding Out About Light

Terry Jennings

Illustrations by
Peter Smith and
Catherine Ward

Belitha Press

First published in the United Kingdom in 1995 by
Belitha Press Ltd, London House, Great Eastern Wharf,
Parkgate Road, London SW11 4NQ
First published 1995 by Cynthia Parzych Publishing Inc, New York
Copyright © 1995 Cynthia Parzych Publishing, Inc.

Text copyright © 1995 Terry Jennings

Designed by Arcadia Consultants.

Printed and bound in Spain.

British Library Cataloguing in Publication Data for this book
is available from the British Library.

ISBN 1 85561 501 0

Words in **bold** appear in the glossary on page 31.

PHOTO CREDITS
Art Director's Photo Library: 20
Belitha Press Limited: 23
B & U International Picture Service: 16 bottom, 25
Celstron: 24 centre
© Frank V DeSisto: 18
© Jonathon Eastland: 8 bottom, 16 top, 20, 28
Image Engineering: 13
Jennings, Dr Terry: 8 centre, 14
Lambe, Dr Thomas: 24 top
© 1994 Monterey Bay Aquarium: 8 top
NASA: 6 top
Norfolk Seaport Association: 6 bottom

Contents

What is light?

L ight is all around us. We can see things only when light is shining on them. Without light we cannot see.

In the daytime nearly all our light comes from the Sun. At night most of our light comes from electric lights. Some light also comes from the moon and from the stars.

Warning: Never look directly at the Sun. It could damage your eyes.

The setting Sun

A full moon

Oil lamp

Reading lamp

Room lamp

Desk lamp

Torch

Candle

Light all around us

Most of our light comes from the Sun. **Electricity** can also give us light.

Some of the most powerful electric lamps are in **lighthouses**. Lighthouses warn ships and boats to keep away from rocks. The lamp of a lighthouse has **lenses** all around it. These lenses make the light into a bright, narrow beam. The lenses are turned by electric motors. They make the beam sweep around.

In the past, people called lighthouse keepers looked after lighthouses. They lived in the lighthouse. Today most lighthouses do not have lighthouse keepers. They are run by computers.

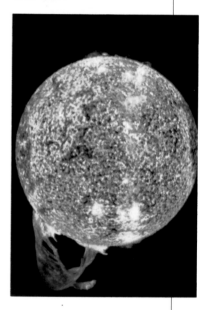
The surface of the Sun

The lighthouse at Sheffield Island

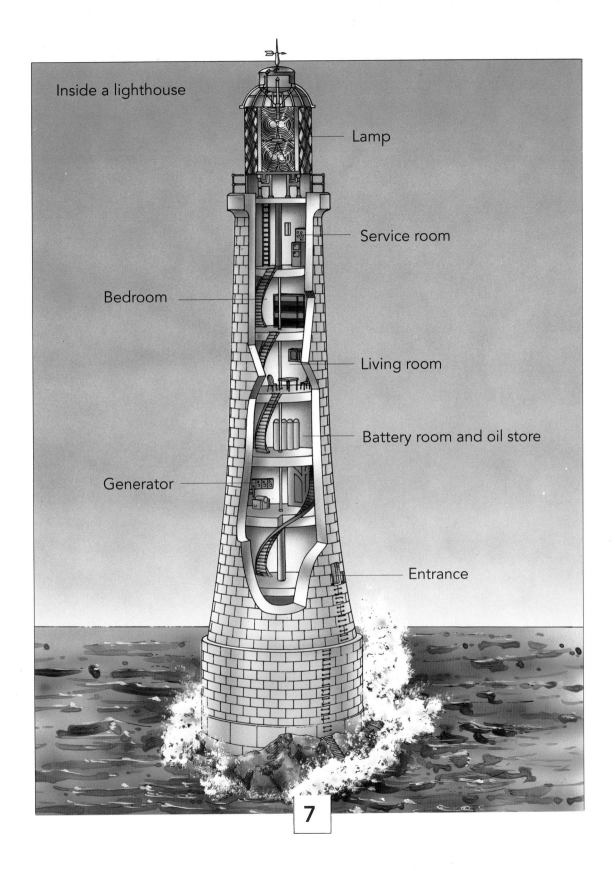

Inside a lighthouse

Lamp

Service room

Bedroom

Living room

Battery room and oil store

Generator

Entrance

What can light pass through?

Sunlight shines through windows. A window is usually made from glass. You can see through a glass window because glass is a **transparent** material. Some materials let through some light. Waxed paper and tissue paper let through a little light. You cannot see through them clearly. Materials like these are **translucent**. Some materials, such as wood, do not let any light through. They are **opaque**.

An aquarium is transparent.

A translucent lampshade

A ship's mast is opaque.

What can you see through?

What to do

1 Make a collection of bottles, bags, cans and jars.

2 Switch on a torch. Put it on a table so that it shines towards you. Hold each container up to the light. Which is transparent, which is translucent and which is opaque?

3 Make a chart of your results.

How does light travel?

Light travels in straight lines called rays. It cannot go around corners. Sometimes in a sunny room you can see specks of dust floating in the air. They are lit up by light moving across the room. You can see the straight path of light. You can see for yourself how light travels.

What to do

1 Find three pieces of thin cardboard, all the same size. Draw lines across each one to find the centre. Ask an adult to make a pencil hole in the centre of each piece.

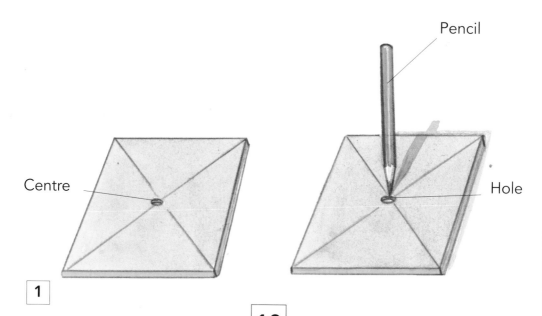

Pencil

Centre

Hole

1

2 Ask an adult to push a knitting needle through the holes to make sure all three pieces of cardboard are in a straight line. Use modelling clay to keep them upright.

3 Stand a piece of black paper behind the last card. Shine a torch through the holes. Where does the light fall?
Move the middle card a little to one side. Shine the torch through the holes. Where does the light fall now?

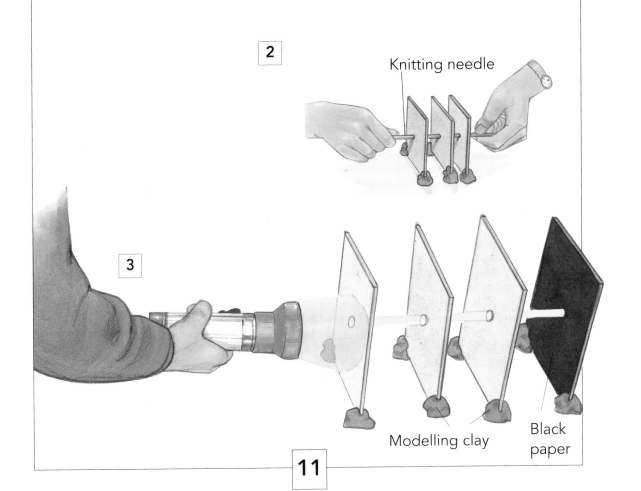

Knitting needle

Modelling clay

Black paper

Lasers

A **laser** sends out a very narrow beam of light. This beam is very powerful. Some laser beams can cut a hole in a thick steel sheet. Some lasers have a crystal, such as a ruby, in them. Others have special dyes or gases. The crystal, dye or gas makes light which comes out of the laser in a narrow beam. Factories use lasers to cut metal, glass or cloth. Doctors use low-powered lasers to carry out delicate operations. Lasers are used in compact disc players and at supermarket checkouts.

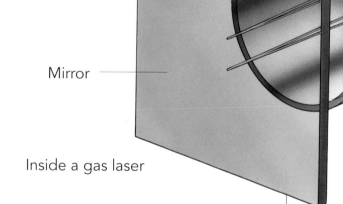

Mirror

Inside a gas laser

Using a laser to cut metal

Lasers create some of the coloured lighting at concerts and stage shows. Laser beams can also be sent along thin glass fibres. They carry radio, television and telephone messages.

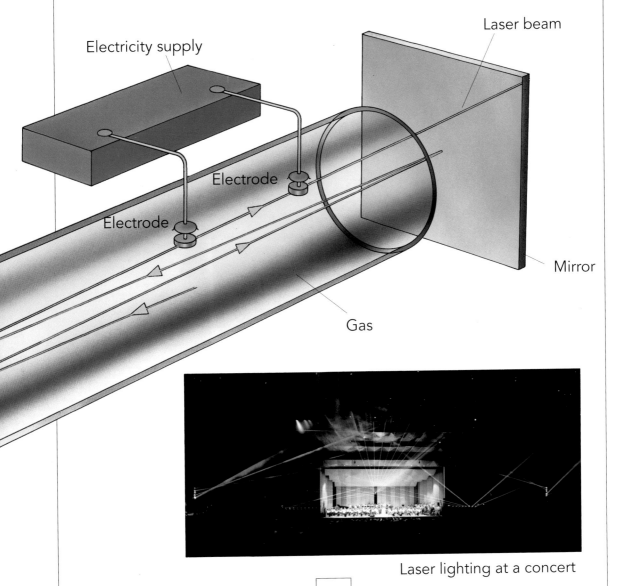

Electricity supply

Laser beam

Electrode

Electrode

Mirror

Gas

Laser lighting at a concert

Light bounces off surfaces, just as a ball bounces off a wall. This is called **reflection**. If a surface is rough, like a brick, light bounces off in all directions. If a surface is smooth and shiny, it can be used as a **mirror**. In a mirror we can see the images or reflections of things held in front of it.

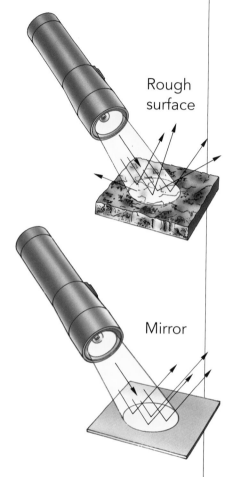

Rough surface

Mirror

Mirrors are usually made from smooth glass. Behind this is a thin layer of shiny metal. A mirror shows us what we look like. Cars have mirrors so that drivers can see behind them.

A swan reflected in still water.

What to do

1 Collect a group of shiny things such as saucepans, spoons, kitchen foil and decorations.

2 Look for the shiny surfaces of each. Can you see your face in any of them? Does your face look the same in each object?

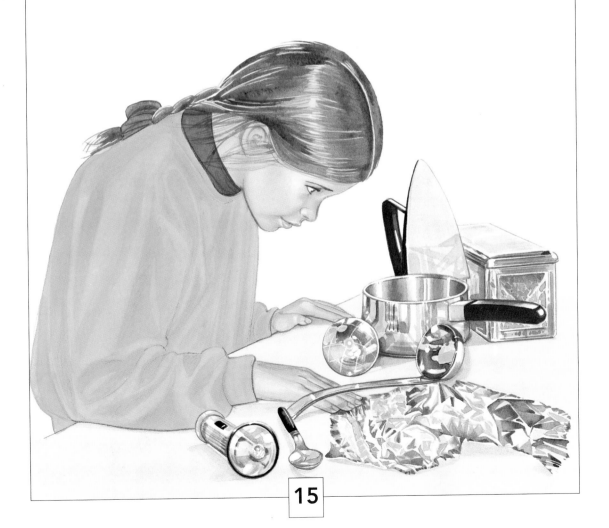

A flat mirror does not show you as you really are. Your image in a mirror is reversed. If you wink your right eye, your reflection winks the left eye. If you touch your left ear, your reflection touches the right ear. If you write your name on a piece of paper, the mirror reverses the writing.

A convex mirror

Not all mirrors are flat. Convex mirrors bulge outwards. They make things look smaller but give a wider view. Car mirrors are convex mirrors. Concave mirrors curve inwards. They make things that are near look bigger.

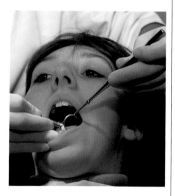

A dentist uses a concave mirror.

Make a kaleidescope

What to do

1 Join three flat mirrors with tape. The shiny sides should face each other.
2 Drop tiny pieces of tin foil and coloured paper between them.
3 Look inside. What do you see?

A shiny spoon can be a curved mirror. Look at yourself in both sides of a shiny spoon. Are the reflections the same?

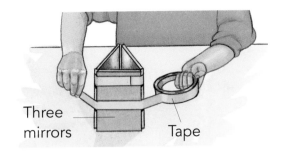

Three mirrors

Tape

1

Foil

2

3

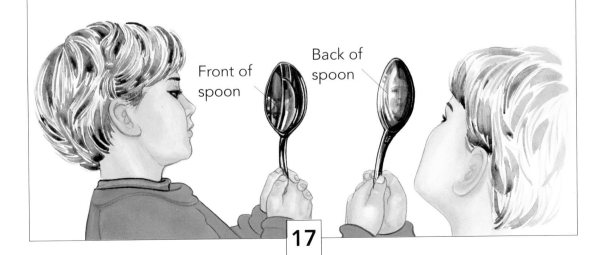

Front of spoon

Back of spoon

Periscopes

Sometimes it is useful for us to see over the top of things. A periscope lets you do this.

A periscope is a hollow tube which has a mirror at each end. The periscope can be raised or lowered.

Submarines have periscopes. The crew can use the periscope to see what is happening on the water's surface. They can do this even while the submarine is underwater.

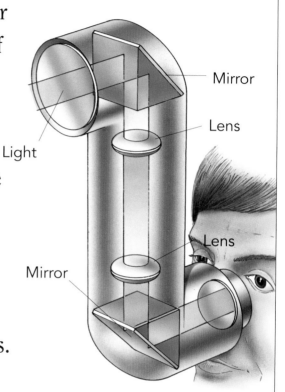

Mirror

Lens

Light

Lens

Mirror

Inside a periscope

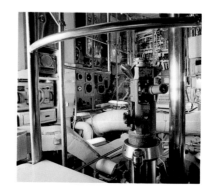

A periscope inside a submarine

Make a periscope

What to do

1 Find a cardboard tube. Ask an adult to help you make two holes in the tube, as shown.

2 Now cut two slots in the tube. Slide two mirrors into the slots.

3 Seal the end of the tube with black paper or plastic.

4 Now look through your periscope. What do you see?

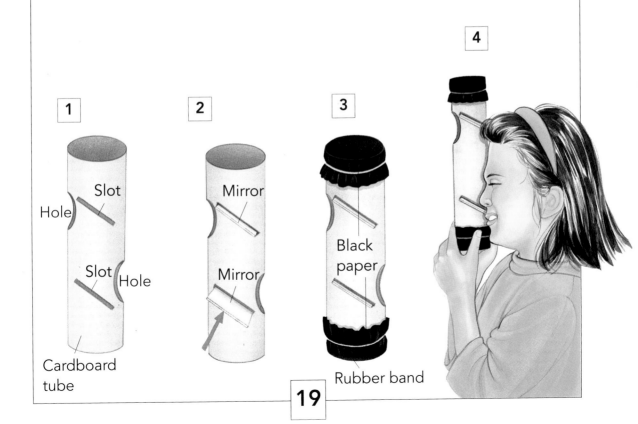

Everything that is in light is bright. A **shadow** is a dark area. It is made when something blocks out the light. The shape of a shadow is roughly the shape of the object or person that made it.

Dark shadows are made by people and objects in bright sunshine.

Make shadows

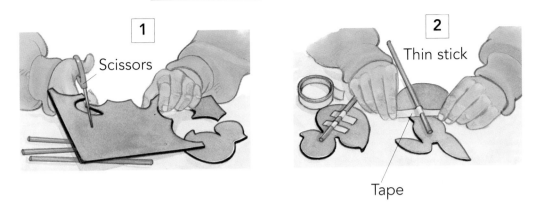

What to do

1 Cut out some shapes from thin cardboard.

2 Tape a thin stick to the back of each shape. Shine the light of a desk lamp on to a wall.

3 Hold the shadow puppets between the lamp and the wall. Look at the shadows made by the different shapes.

Refraction and lenses

Light does not always travel at the same speed. Light moves faster through air than through water. When light changes speed, it usually also changes direction slightly. This makes things seem to bend. This is why a straw in a glass of water looks bent. This bending of light is called **refraction**. Lenses work because of refraction. This is because light travels slower through glass than through air.

Drinking straw

A convex lens is thicker in the middle. It bends light rays together. A convex lens can be used to make things look bigger. It is often called a magnifying glass.

A concave lens is thicker at the edges. It spreads the light rays apart. If you look through a concave lens, things seem smaller.

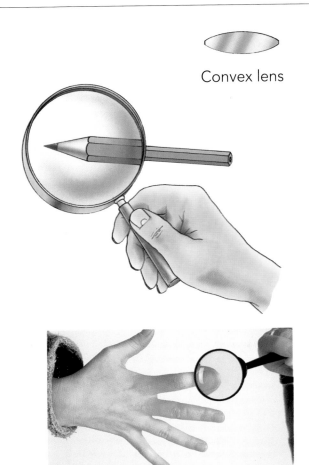

Convex lens

A magnifying glass is a convex lens.

Concave lens

Telescopes, binoculars and microscopes

We have a convex lens in each eye. These lenses help us to see. Glasses, **telescopes**, **binoculars** and **cameras** have lenses in them too. Binoculars work like two small telescopes, one for each eye.

Glasses have lenses.

Using binoculars

How the eye works

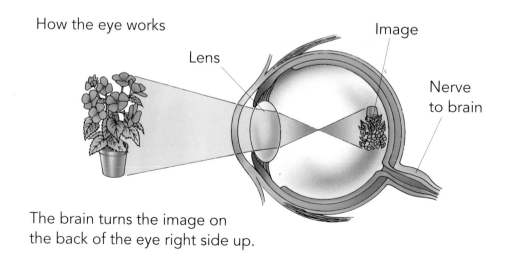

The brain turns the image on the back of the eye right side up.

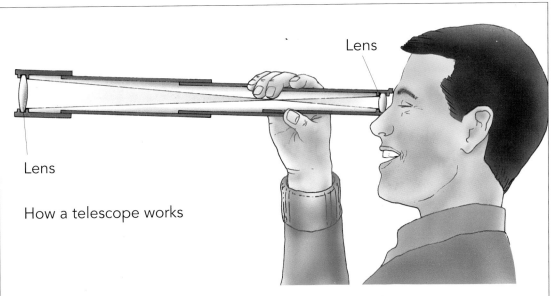

Lens

Lens

How a telescope works

A simple telescope has two lenses. They make things seem closer. A large lens at the front bends the light rays together. The rays make an image and a small lens makes the image larger.

A **microscope** also uses lenses to bend light. Some microscopes have many lenses. A microscope using light can make things seem up to 2 000 times bigger.

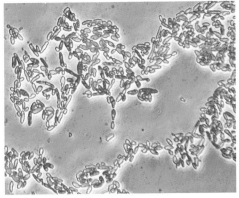

A microscope makes things such as these **cells** look bigger.

Experiment with lenses

What to do

1 Find a clear glass jar with a screw-on lid.
2 Fill the jar with water and screw the lid on tightly. Hold it over a newspaper.
3 Look at the words in the newspaper. Do they look bigger? The jar of water is acting as a convex lens or magnifying glass.

Jar of water

What to do

You can use a drop of water as a simple lens.
1 Find a clear plastic lid.
2 Make a small hole in it with a drawing pin. Cover the hole with one drop of water.
3 Hold it over the newspaper and look through the drop. Does your lens make the words seem bigger?

Lid

Drop of water

Make a telescope

What to do

1 Take two magnifying glasses.

2 Hold one magnifying glass in each hand.

3 Look through the two lenses together. Can you make things look bigger or smaller?

4 Change the distance between the magnifying glasses. What differences do you see?

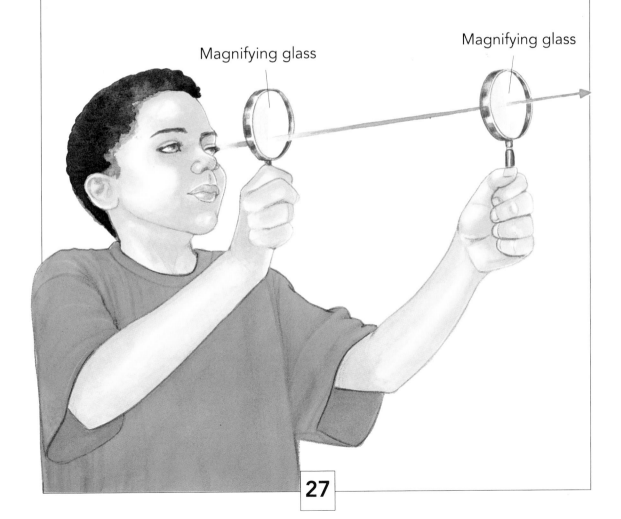

Magnifying glass

Magnifying glass

Cameras

Cameras are used to take pictures called photographs. The front of a camera has a lens. They make an image appear on the film inside the camera. When you look into the viewfinder, you see the picture the camera will take. When you press the button to take the photograph, the shutter opens like a little door. The shutter opens for only a fraction of a second. It lets a little light on to the film. There are chemicals on the film which are changed by the light.

Taking a photograph

The chemicals on the film store the image. When the film is developed, you can see the images. Photographs are printed from the film.

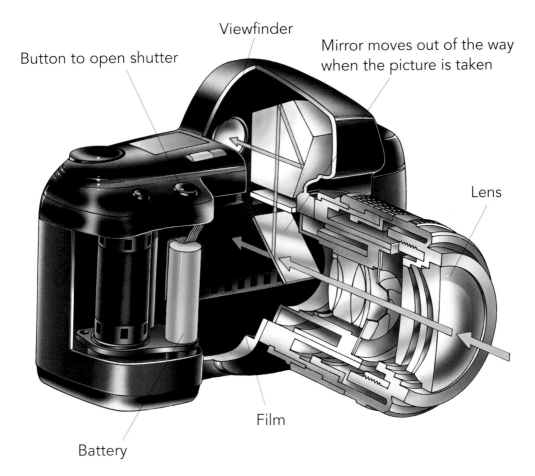

Viewfinder

Button to open shutter

Mirror moves out of the way when the picture is taken

Lens

Film

Battery

Inside a camera

Make a pinhole camera

The first camera did not have a lens. It was a box with a tiny hole in the side. Light passed through the hole. It made an upside-down image inside the box.

What to do

1 Cut a hole in one end of a shoebox. Paint the inside of the box black. Let the paint dry.

2 Cover the hole with tracing paper to make a window. Use a pin to make a tiny hole in the other end.

3 Put the lid on the box. Hold the camera up to your eyes.

4 Point the pinhole at a table lamp. What can you see on the tracing paper?

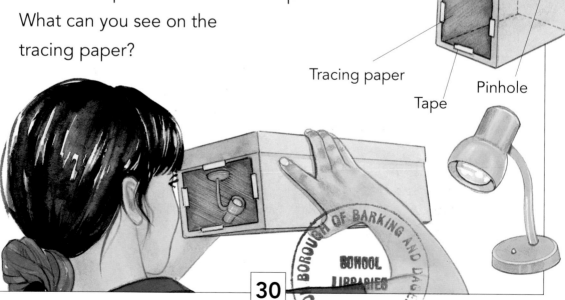

Shoebox

Tracing paper

Tape

Pinhole

Glossary

Binoculars An instrument with lenses for both eyes that make distant objects look nearer.

Camera A device for taking photographs.

Cells Very small parts of living things. There are many different kinds of cell. Each cell has a special job to do in the body of a plant or animal.

Electricity A form of **energy** that can be changed to light, heat, sound or movement energy.

Energy Something needed to change things or make things move. Light, sound, heat and electricity are forms of energy.

Kaleidoscope A tube which has mirrors inside. You see colourful patterns when you look in it.

Laser A device that sends out a narrow beam of powerful light.

Lens A curved piece of glass or clear plastic. Some lenses make things look bigger.

Light The Sun and stars give off light. Light is the opposite of dark.

Lighthouse A tower with a bright, flashing light to guide and warn ships.

Magnifying glass A lens that makes objects look bigger.

Microscope An instrument that makes tiny things look larger.

Mirror A smooth glass or metal surface that reflects things.

Opaque Describes a material that does not let through light.

Reflection What happens to light when it hits something and bounces off it.

Refraction The way in which rays of light change direction slightly when they pass from one substance to another.

Shadow A dark shape formed when an object blocks light.

Telescope An instrument with a lens for one eye that makes distant objects look clearer.

Translucent Describes a material that lets through some light but not enough to see through it.

Transparent Describes something which you can see through.

Index